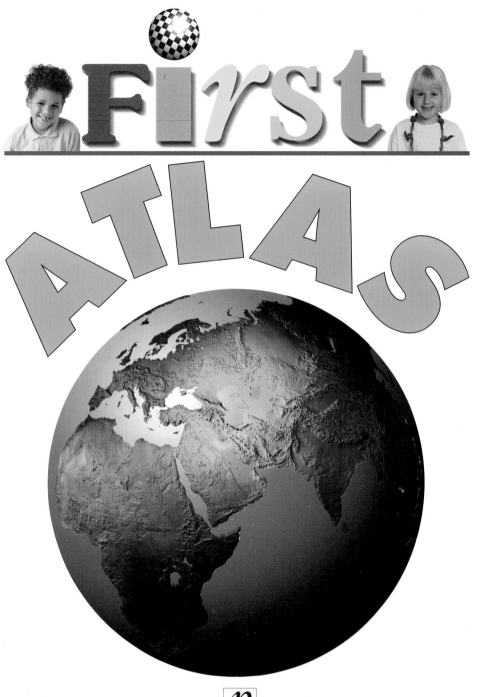

First ATLAS

p

Author
John Grisewood

Cover Design
Miles Kelly Publishing Ltd.

This is a Parragon Book
This edition published in 2001

Parragon
Queen Street House
4 Queen Street
Bath BA1 1HE, UK

British Library Cataloguing-in-Publication Data

A catalogue record for this book is available from the British Library.

ISBN 0-75255-986-9

Printed in Italy

 Elk

 Turtle

 Barbary ape

 Dairy cows

 Beef cattle

 Sheep

 Penguin

 Panda

 Bactrian camel

 Rice

 Cotton

 Wheat

 Grapes

 Fir trees

 Palm trees

 Cactus

 Container ship

 Passenger ferry

 Oil tanker

 Trawler

 Fishing boats

 Reed boat

 Gondola

 Tractor

 Yacht

 Football

 Horse racing

 Surfing

 Skiing

 Oil rig

 Factory

 Windmill

 Canal scene

 City skyline

 Volcano

 Gt Wall, China

Mountain peak

Pig

Poultry

Maize

Rainforest

Sand dunes

Tourism

Icons
These little pictures on the maps give you all sorts of extra information about a country. Some of them show buildings. Others show landscapes, animals or plants. Some show the kind of work people do, or how they spend their free time.

Contents

Introduction

Earth Facts

The world we live in is a planet, a huge ball of rock which flies through space. It is called Earth. The Earth travels around our local star, which is called the Sun. As it travels, it spins round and round. It stays on course because it is pulled towards the Sun by a force called gravity. The Earth is one of nine planets which circle the Sun. It is also the only planet on which living things are known to exist.

When we see pictures of Earth taken from out in space, it looks beautiful. We can see the bright blue of the oceans. We can see the brown of the rocks and soil that make up big areas of land. These are called continents. We can see swirling white patterns, too. These are clouds, made up of tiny drops of water. They float in the air which surrounds the planet. Air and water make it possible for us to live on Earth.

Deserts are very dry areas of rock, stones or sand. This desert is part of **Death Valley**, in the USA.

High mountain ranges are covered by snow and ice. These are the **Andes** mountains, in South America.

The giant clam is one of the fascinating and varied sorts of sea life found on the **Great Barrier Reef**, off the coast of Queensland in Australia.

What is a map?

A map is a plan showing the planet's surface. The Earth's surface is curved, so it can only be shown properly on a round globe. Maps are normally on paper, and so the surface has to be shown as if it were flat.

Many maps show the lie of the land. You can see which areas are low and which are high. You can pick out mountain peaks, coasts and rivers, lakes and seas. These are called natural features. Some maps just show the borders of countries, states and provinces. Some show cities, roads and railway lines. The maps in this atlas show the land and coastlines as well as national borders and cities.

Spot the mountain
Maps use little badges called symbols. A small black triangle means 'mountain'. Look for the name of the peak and its height in metres above sea level. Other symbols are shown below.

Read the map
This map is of Japan. What are the names of the four main islands? Is the land mostly flat or mountainous?

HOKKAIDO

Kuril Is. (Russia)

Asahi Mt. 2,290 m

Sapporo

Kitakami

Sendai

JAPAN

HONSHU

Mito

Tokyo

Yokohama

Kyoto Nagoya

Kobe

Osaka

Mt. Fuji 3,776 m

Hiroshima

Kitakyushu

Fukuoka

SHIKOKU

Kii Channel

PACIFIC OCEAN

KYUSHU

Towns and cities
Towns and cities are shown by round dots. Each country's chief city, or capital, is shown by a square.

Where in the world?
Look for the little round maps to see just where each map fits on to the globe as a whole

Key to symbols

capital city	■
city or town	●
mountain	▲
national border	—
coastline	
river	
lake	■
highlands	
plains	■

5

Countries of the World

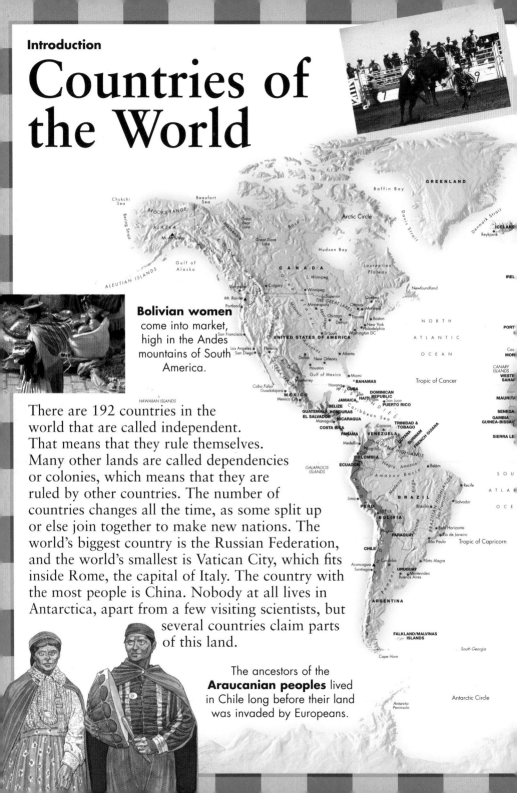

Bolivian women come into market, high in the Andes mountains of South America.

There are 192 countries in the world that are called independent. That means that they rule themselves. Many other lands are called dependencies or colonies, which means that they are ruled by other countries. The number of countries changes all the time, as some split up or else join together to make new nations. The world's biggest country is the Russian Federation, and the world's smallest is Vatican City, which fits inside Rome, the capital of Italy. The country with the most people is China. Nobody at all lives in Antarctica, apart from a few visiting scientists, but several countries claim parts of this land.

The ancestors of the **Araucanian peoples** lived in Chile long before their land was invaded by Europeans.

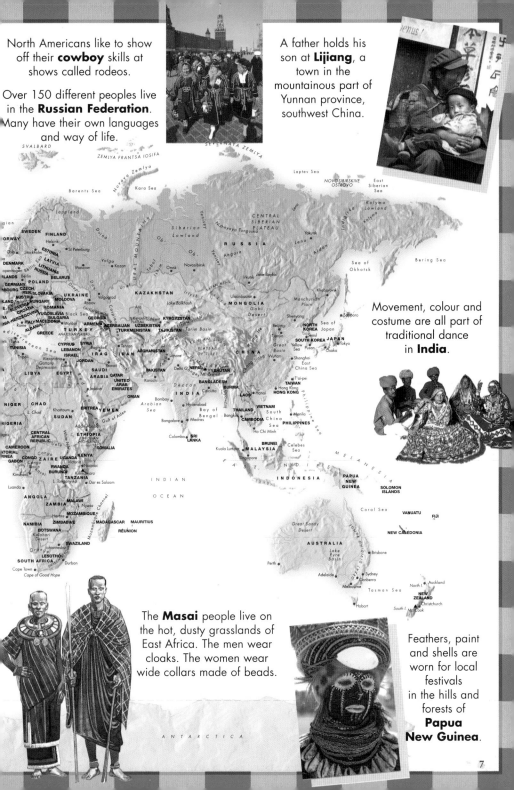

North Americans like to show off their **cowboy** skills at shows called rodeos.

A father holds his son at **Lijiang**, a town in the mountainous part of Yunnan province, southwest China.

Over 150 different peoples live in the **Russian Federation**. Many have their own languages and way of life.

Movement, colour and costume are all part of traditional dance in **India**.

The **Masai** people live on the hot, dusty grasslands of East Africa. The men wear cloaks. The women wear wide collars made of beads.

Feathers, paint and shells are worn for local festivals in the hills and forests of **Papua New Guinea**.

7

Scandinavia and Finland

The Baltic and the North Sea are divided by two long arms of the European mainland, which together are known as Scandinavia. The southern arm is called Jutland. Along with several large islands it makes up a country called Denmark. This land is flat and green. Its farms produce butter and bacon.

The other long arm of land stretches down from the Arctic. Its coastline is ragged, with deep sea inlets called fjords in the west. Mountains run down from north to south. There are big forests and thousands of lakes, sparkling blue in summer, but frozen over during the harsh northern winter. The western lands belong to Norway and the eastern lands to Sweden. Oil is taken from beneath the North Sea, metals from the land and timber from the forests. The eastern shores of the Baltic Sea are taken up by Finland, a land of forests and lakes stretching to the borders of Russia.

These soldiers are on duty outside **Amalienborg Castle** in **Denmark**. Their job is to guard the life of the Danish queen.

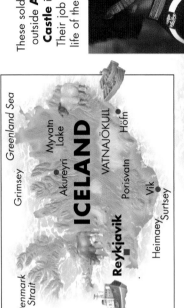

Greenland Sea

Denmark Strait

Grimsey

Myvatn Lake

Akureyri

ICELAND

VATNAJÖKULL

Höfn

Porisvatn

Vik

Surtsey

Heimaey

Reykjavik

RUSSIA

North Cape

Hammerfest

LAPLAND

Luleå

Oulu

Kiruna

Mt. Kebnekaise 2,111m

Narvik

LOFOTEN VESTERÄLEN

FINLAND

Kuopio

Tampere

Turku

Helsinki

Pleasure boats are tied up at a jetty on the **Aura river in Turku**. This city is a busy seaport on the Gulf of Bothnia, in southern Finland. It was once the capital of the country, but today the chief city is Helsinki, to the east.

Gulf of Bothnia

ÅLAND

SWEDEN

Uppsala

Stockholm

GOTLAND

Västervik

Linköping

Vättern

ÖLAND

Jönköping

BALTIC SEA

Vänern

Bornholm

Göteborg

Malmö

NORWAY

Trondheim

Galdhøpiggen
2,469m

Bergen

Oslo

Stavanger

DENMARK

Kattegat

Skagerr

Århus

Horsens

Copenhagen

GERMANY

Many Scandinavian fairy tales are about **trolls**. These strange creatures are said to be giants or dwarfs, who live in caves.

NORWEGIAN SEA

The **Saami people** live in the far north, in a region called Lapland. They keep herds of reindeer. This woman is weaving cloth.

Low Countries

The Netherlands and Belgium border the North Sea and are very low lying. For hundreds of years the people there have fought against floods and storms. They have learned to fill in coastal areas to make new farmland, called polder.

The lands near the coast are flat and green, drained by canals and by great rivers such as the Rhine, the Schelde and the Meuse. Windmills were once used to pump out the wet fields, and may still be seen today. In southern Belgium the land rises to a chain of wooded hills called the Ardennes. These stretch southwards into Luxembourg, a tiny country with rich farmland.

The Netherlands is famous for its cheeses, its vegetables, cut flowers and electrical goods. Belgium produces steel and machinery. Luxembourg produces wine and is a centre of business.

The lowlands region is home to several peoples including Frisians, Dutch, Flemings and Walloons.

Amsterdam, the capital of the Netherlands, is built around a network of canals. The Prinsengracht runs through the old part of the city, which was built in the 1600s.

Alkmaar is a town in the North Holland region of the Netherlands. Tourists like to visit its famous **cheese market**, and watch the big, round cheeses being carried out and weighed.

This is the **Atomium**, a strange-looking landmark in Brussels, the capital of Belgium. It was built forty years ago for a big international fair.

NETHERLANDS

Groningen

West Frisian Islands

Waddenzee

IJsselmeer

Haarlem ■ **Amsterdam**

Enschede

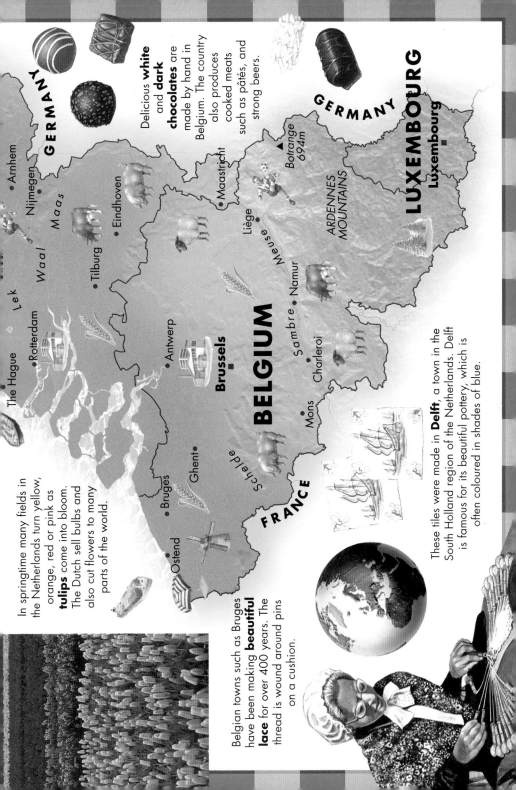

GERMANY

GERMANY

LUXEMBOURG

Luxembourg

FRANCE

BELGIUM

Botrange
694m

ARDENNES
MOUNTAINS

• Arnhem

• Nijmegen

Maas

• Eindhoven

• Tilburg

Waal

Lek

• Rotterdam

The Hague

• Maastricht

• Liège

Meuse

• Namur

Sambre

Antwerp •

Brussels

• Charleroi

• Mons

Scheldte

Ghent•

• Bruges

• Ostend

Delicious **white** and **dark chocolates** are made by hand in Belgium. The country also produces cooked meats such as pâtés, and strong beers.

In springtime many fields in the Netherlands turn yellow, orange, red or pink as **tulips** come into bloom. The Dutch sell bulbs and also cut flowers to many parts of the world.

Belgian towns such as Bruges have been making **beautiful lace** for over 400 years. The thread is wound around pins on a cushion.

These tiles were made in **Delft**, a town in the South Holland region of the Netherlands. Delft is famous for its beautiful pottery, which is often coloured in shades of blue.

British Isles

The British Isles lie off the mainland of Europe. Ocean currents and winds keep the weather mild and moist. The largest island is Great Britain, which is made up of three countries joined together in a United Kingdom. These are England, Scotland and Wales. The second biggest island is called Ireland. The northern part of this is governed as part of the United Kingdom, but most of it is a separate country called the Republic of Ireland.

England has rich farmland in the south and bleak moors in the north. Both Scotland and Wales include highlands where sheep or cattle are raised. Many islands lie to the west and to the north of Scotland. There are many large cities in Great Britain. The biggest of all is London, on the River Thames. The Irish capital is called Dublin. Ireland is a land of green fields, peat bogs, mountains and rivers.

Bagpipes are played in the highlands of Scotland. Pipe music can be sad or stirring. Bagpipes are sometimes used by pop bands as well as by traditional pipers.

This brightly painted **longboat** is on the River Wey, in the southeast of England. Longboats like these were once used to transport pottery and other factory goods. Today they are mostly used for holiday cruises.

SHETLAND ISLANDS

ORKNEY ISLANDS

John o'Groats

NORTH SEA

Peterhead

Aberdeen

Inverness

Loch Ness

Dundee

Perth

NORTH WEST

Ben Nevis 1,343 m

Mallaig

Forth

Glasgow • Edinburgh

Ayr

SCOTLAND

Newcastle upon Tyne

Lewis

Skye

OUTER HEBRIDES

INNER HEBRIDES

Islay

Londonderry

ATLANTIC OCEAN

NORTHERN IRELAND

Donegal • Belfast

Dublin

IRELAND

Limerick •

Killarney •

Waterford •

Cork •

Middlesbrough •

Kingston upon Hull •

LINCOLN WOLDS

Blackpool • Leeds •

Morecambe •

Manchester •

Liverpool •

Sheffield •

PENNINES

ENGLAND

Norwich •

Chelmsford •

Southend-on-Sea

London

Canterbury

Dover

Thames

Brighton

Oxford •

Reading •

Birmingham • Coventry •

Severn

Isle of Wight

ENGLISH CHANNEL

CAMBRIAN

WALES

Bristol •

Cardiff •

Swansea •

Southampton •

EXMOOR

Exeter •

Plymouth •

Penzance •

ISLES OF SCILLY

Isle of Man

IRISH SEA

Lobster pots are piled up on the quay at Dingle, alongside fishing boats. Ireland's Atlantic coast has small islands, peaceful rivers and high cliffs pounded by the ocean.

CHANNEL ISLANDS

Green farmland fringes moors, forests and mountains in the **Brecon Beacons National Park**, in Wales.

13

France and Monaco

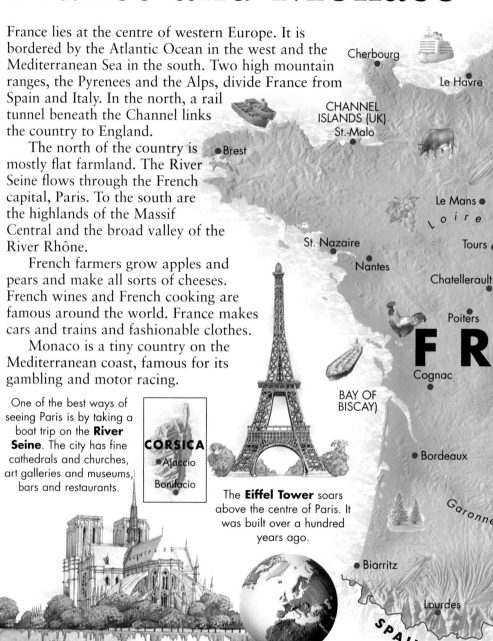

France lies at the centre of western Europe. It is bordered by the Atlantic Ocean in the west and the Mediterranean Sea in the south. Two high mountain ranges, the Pyrenees and the Alps, divide France from Spain and Italy. In the north, a rail tunnel beneath the Channel links the country to England.

The north of the country is mostly flat farmland. The River Seine flows through the French capital, Paris. To the south are the highlands of the Massif Central and the broad valley of the River Rhône.

French farmers grow apples and pears and make all sorts of cheeses. French wines and French cooking are famous around the world. France makes cars and trains and fashionable clothes.

Monaco is a tiny country on the Mediterranean coast, famous for its gambling and motor racing.

One of the best ways of seeing Paris is by taking a boat trip on the **River Seine**. The city has fine cathedrals and churches, art galleries and museums, bars and restaurants.

The **Eiffel Tower** soars above the centre of Paris. It was built over a hundred years ago.

Cherbourg

Le Havre

CHANNEL ISLANDS (UK)

St.-Malo

Brest

Le Mans

Loire

St. Nazaire

Tours

Nantes

Chatellerault

Poiters

F R

Cognac

BAY OF BISCAY)

CORSICA

Ajaccio

Bonifacio

Bordeaux

Garonne

Biarritz

Lourdes

SPAIN

Vines are being pruned in Alsace, a part of France that borders Germany. French grapes produce some of the world's best wines.

Calais
Boulogne
Lille
ieppe
uen
Seine
Reims
Paris
Marne
Meuse
Moselle
Nancy
Strasbourg
Rhine
artres
Orléans
Loire
Saône
BELGIUM
LUXEMBOURG
GERMANY

Haute cuisine means high-quality cooking. French families love to eat well, either at home or in a restatuarant.

mussels
chicken
snails

SWITZERLAND

ANCE

imoges
Clermont-Ferrand
Lyon
Saône
Rhône
Mont Blanc 4,807m

MASSIF CENTRAL

fruit tart

dogne
Lot
Lot
Rhône
Grenoble

ALPS

ITALY

cheese

Avignon
Montpellier
oulouse

MONACO
Nice
Cannes

Marseille
Toulon

Perpignan
ANDORRA

Many rich people tie up their yachts at **Monte Carlo**, in Monaco. French ports such as Cannes and Nice also attract wealthy tourists.

Germany and the Alps

Three small countries take in most of western Europe's highest mountain range, the Alps. They are Switzerland, Liechtenstein and Austria. Here, snowy peaks and rivers of ice tower over green valleys, dark forests and deep lakes. Wooden houses stand in Alpine meadows. They are covered with snow in winter, but are bright with flowers in summer. Languages spoken in the Alps include German, French, Romansh and Italian.

The Alps stretch northwards into southern Germany. Germany is a large country which lies at the heart of Europe. It has forests and steep river valleys, rolling heath and flat plains. Sandy coasts border the North Sea and the Baltic Sea. Germany has many big cities, with factories producing cars, chemical and electrical goods, but it also has pretty villages dating back to the Middle Ages. The German language is spoken throughout, but with many different accents.

The **Matterhorn** is a great needle of rock and ice. It rises in the Swiss Alps, near the Italian border.

NORTH SEA

EAST FRISIAN

Hamburg

Bremen

Weser

Hannover   All

HARZ MT

Rhine   Dortmund
        Essen
Düsseldorf
    Cologne (Köln)

Bonn

GERMA

Rhine   Frankfurt am Main

FRANCE

Rhine   BLACK FOREST   Stuttgart

Lake Constance (Bodensee)

Zurich

LIECHTENSTEI
            Vaduz

Bern
SWITZERLAND

ALPS

Lake Geneva

Geneva

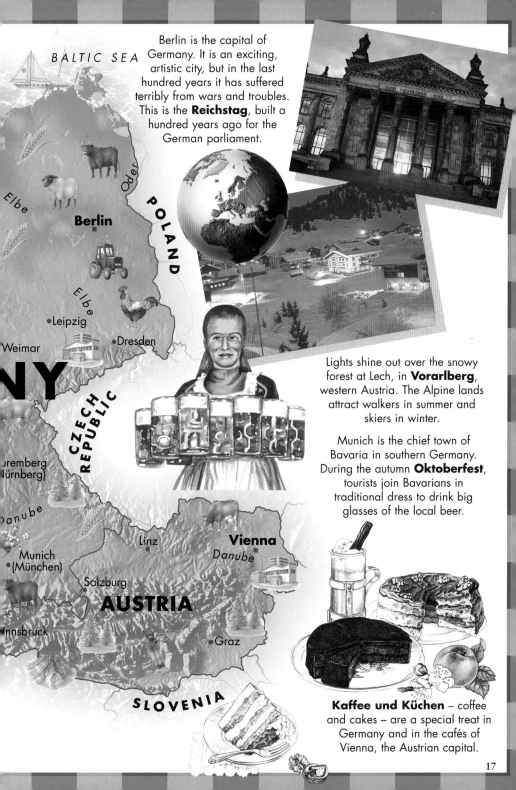

BALTIC SEA

Berlin is the capital of Germany. It is an exciting, artistic city, but in the last hundred years it has suffered terribly from wars and troubles. This is the **Reichstag**, built a hundred years ago for the German parliament.

Elbe

Berlin

P O L A N D

Oder

Elbe

•Leipzig

•Dresden

Weimar

NY

C Z E C H R E P U B L I C

Lights shine out over the snowy forest at Lech, in **Vorarlberg**, western Austria. The Alpine lands attract walkers in summer and skiers in winter.

Munich is the chief town of Bavaria in southern Germany. During the autumn **Oktoberfest**, tourists join Bavarians in traditional dress to drink big glasses of the local beer.

uremberg (Nürnberg)

Danube

Linz

Vienna
Danube

Munich (München)

Salzburg

AUSTRIA

Innsbruck

•Graz

S L O V E N I A

Kaffee und Küchen – coffee and cakes – are a special treat in Germany and in the cafés of Vienna, the Austrian capital.

Spain and Portugal

The Iberian peninsula is a great block of land which juts out into the Atlantic Ocean. It is ringed by the snowy mountains of the Pyrenees, the Cantabrian ranges and the Sierra Nevada. Much of it is dry and hot in summer. Rivers cross the western plains and flow into the Atlantic.

The region grows grapes for wine, olives, oranges and cork. There are large fishing fleets. Factories produce cars and leather goods. Many tourists spend their holidays on the coasts.

There are three nations on the Iberian peninsula. The smallest is Andorra, high in the Pyrenees. Portugal, in the west, is a beautiful country with its own language. The largest country is Spain. Here, Spanish is spoken everywhere, but a number of other peoples have their own languages and way of life, including the Basques, Galicians and Catalans. A fourth piece of land, Gibraltar in the far south, is a British colony.

Bay of Biscay

La Coruña
Gijón
CANTABRIAN

CAPE FINISTERRE

Vigo

Valladolid

Porto
Douro

PORTUGAL

Coimbra

Tajo

Tagus

Lisbon

Guadiana

Córdoba

Seville • Guadalquivir

Gulf of Cadiz
A thousand years ago, Arab peoples from North Africa ruled most of Spain. They were Moslems and built beautiful **mosques** such as this one in Cordoba.

Cádiz
Gibraltar (U.K.)
Strait of Gibralta

18

Ronda is a small town of white houses in Andalucía, in southern Spain. It is built on the edge of towering cliffs which are linked by high bridges.

FRANCE

PYRENEES

MOUNTAINS

ANDORRA
Andorra la Vella

Bilbao

Vitoria   Pamplona

Ebro

Duero   Saragossa

Barcelona

SPAIN

Madrid

Menorca

Mallorca
Palma

Valencia

Ibiza
Ibiza

adiana

La Carolina
Linares

Alicante

Murcia

Granada

Spanish girls in traditional costume enjoy all the fun of the fair. Spain has many festivals called **fiestas**. Many of these celebrate Christian saints' days.

MEDITERRANEAN SEA

Portuguese food includes delicious seafood dishes, sardines, fruits and wines. The drink port takes its name from the town of Oporto.

19

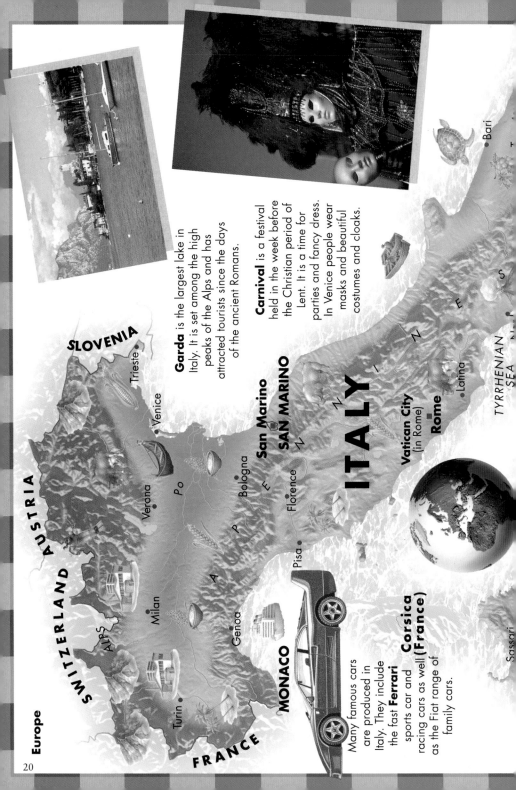

SLOVENIA

SWITZERLAND **AUSTRIA**

FRANCE

MONACO

ITALY

SAN MARINO

San Marino

Vatican City
(in Rome)

Rome

ALPS

Turin

Milan

Verona

Venice

Trieste

Genoa

Po

Pisa

Bologna

Florence

Latina

Bari

Sassari

Corsica **(France)**

TYRRHENIAN
SEA

A P E N N I N E S

Garda is the largest lake in
Italy. It is set among the high
peaks of the Alps and has
attracted tourists since the days
of the ancient Romans.

Carnival is a festival
held in the week before
the Christian period of
Lent. It is a time for
parties and fancy dress.
In Venice people wear
masks and beautiful
costumes and cloaks.

Many famous cars
are produced in
Italy. They include
the fast **Ferrari**
sports car and
racing cars as well
as the Fiat range of
family cars.

Italy and its Neighbours

Italy is a long strip of land stretching into the Mediterranean Sea. In the north are the Alps, a range of high mountains. Below these is a wide plain, crossed by the River Po.

The Appenine mountains run down the centre of the country. Southern Italy includes large areas of dry scrubland. Volcanoes and earthquakes are common. Italy also includes the islands of Sicily and Sardinia.

Italy is the world's biggest wine producer and also exports many foods, including pasta, sauces, olives and salami sausages. Factories in the north produce cars, clothes and leather goods.

Inside Italy there are two other countries, tiny San Marino and also Vatican City, headquarters of the Roman Catholic Church. Another small country, Malta, lies to the south of Sicily.

SARDINIA

Cagliari

Pisa is a town on the River Arno, in the Italian region of Tuscany. Medieval buildings around the central square include a cathedral, a building for baptisms and a famous bell tower which leans over sideways!

LIPARI ISLANDS

● Palermo

SICILY

Catania ●

IONIAN SEA

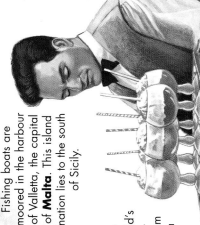

Fishing boats are moored in the harbour of Valletta, the capital of **Malta**. This island nation lies to the south of Sicily.

Italy is famous for making some of world's most delicious ice-creams. An ice-cream parlour is called a **gelateria**.

Central Europe

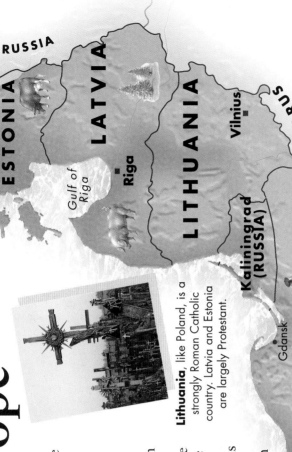

Three small countries border the Baltic Sea. Estonia, Latvia and Lithuania include large areas of forest, bog and open farmland. Until the 1990s these Baltic lands were a part of Russia, which was then called the Soviet Union. Poland, to the south, is a much larger country, lying on a wide open plain between Germany in the west and Belarus and Ukraine in the east. In the south are wooded hills and the high peaks of the Tatra mountains, on the Slovakian border. The Czech and the Slovak republics include rugged mountains and rich farmland. The River Danube flows along the Czech border and through the plains of central Hungary.

Central Europe has warm summers but cold, snowy winters. Industries include machinery, cars, mining, and the making of beers, wines and jams. More and more tourists come to visit beautiful old cities such as Krakow, Prague and Budapest.

Lithuania, like Poland, is a strongly Roman Catholic country. Latvia and Estonia are largely Protestant.

RUSSIA

Gulf of Finland

ESTONIA

Tallinn

Gulf of Riga

LATVIA

Riga

LITHUANIA

Vilnius

BELARUS

Kaliningrad (RUSSIA)

POLAND

Gdansk

Poznan

Vistula

Warsaw

Lodz

Shoppers buy vegetables from a **market stall** in Prague. Central European farms produce wheat, potatoes, barley, maize, sugar beet and sunflowers.

GERMANY

Wroclaw

Vistula

Krakow

Prague

CZECH REPUBLIC

AUSTRIA

SLOVAK REPUBLIC

Bratislava

Budapest

HUNGARY

ROMANIA

Over 1,000 years ago, **Wenceslas** ruled Bohemia, which is now part of the Czech Republic. His statue may be seen in Prague. He is remembered in the words of a Christmas carol, *Good King Wenceslas.*

This fine old **tall ship** is from Poland. It is used for training young sailors. The Baltic Sea has been a centre of trade for thousands of years.

These women are wearing **Estonian costume.** Estonia has been ruled by many other countries over the ages, but has managed to keep up its old traditions.

Goulash is a dish that was first made in Hungary. It is a beef stew flavoured with spicy red pepper and sour cream.

23

Europe

The son of an Albanian farmer shows off his favourite cow. **Albania** is a small, mountainous country on the Adriatic coast.

It is time to make hay on this **Romanian farm**. Everyone in the family lends a hand. The hay will be fed to the animals during the cold months of winter.

The **Parthenon** is a splendid temple, built in the days of the ancient Greeks. It still towers over Athens, the capital city of Greece.

UKRAINE

Iasi

Cluj-Napoca

Tîrgu Mures

Alba Iulia

ROMANIA

Timisoara

Brasov

Moldoveanu ▲
2,543 m

Ljubljana

SLOVENIA

HUNGARY

Drava

Tisz

TRANSYLVANIAN ALPS

Zagreb

CROATIA

Osijek

Kupa

Sava

VOJVODINA

Belgrade

Bucharest

**BOSNIA -
HERZEGOVINA**

Smederevo

Sarajevo

DINARIC ALPS

Split

YUGOSLAVIA SERBIA

BALKAN MOUNTAINS

Kamchiy

MONTENEGRO

Sofia

Kazanluk

Dubrovnik Podgorica KOSOVO

BULGARIA

Lake Scutari

Stara Zagora

Skopje

Plovdiv

MACEDONIA

Tiranë

ALBANIA

Thessaloníki

▲ Mt Olympus
2,917 m

Corfu

GREECE

Lesbos

AEGEAN
SEA

Chios

Ándros

Sámos

Athens

Náxos

Thíra

Cythera

SEA OF CRETE

Iráklion

Crete

Romania and the Balkans

Romania lies on the Black Sea coast. It is a land of mountains and forests. A large triangle of land stretches southwards from Central Europe, ending in chains of islands. It is called the Balkan peninsula and is bordered by the Adriatic, Black and Aegean Seas. The region has rocky mountain ranges and often suffers from earthquakes. Summers are dry and hot. Winters are very cold in the north, but mild in the south. The region produces timber, wines, olives, fruit and dairy products.

Bulgaria lies in the northeast of the peninsula. It has large areas of rich farmland. The northwestern Balkan lands used to be part of one big nation called Yugoslavia, but they now make up five different countries. Greece is the southernmost country of the Balkans and includes many islands. Its ancient villages and fine beaches attract many tourists.

MOUTHS OF THE DANUBE

Constanta

Varna

BLACK SEA

Roses are picked in the Kazanluk region of **Bulgaria**. Their sweet-smelling petals are used to make attar of roses, an oil used in making perfumes.

Zagreb, the capital of **Croatia**, is near the Slovenian border, on the Sava River. The city is on the main route from western Europe to Greece.

Churches, whitewashed villages and blue seas are typical of the Greek lands. This is **Thira**, a volcanic island which is also known as Santorini.

Greek meals might include salad with olives, seafood such as fish or squid, stuffed peppers, beans, a type of wine called retsina and sweet, sticky pastries such as baklava.

Cos

Rhodes

Sunflowers are grown as a crop in many parts of the Balkans. Their seeds may be pressed to make vegetable oil or roasted for eating.

Russian Federation

The Russian Federation is the world's biggest country. It stretches across two continents, Europe and Asia. When the sun is rising in Vladivostok, on the Pacific Coast, it is already setting on the capital, Moscow. In the Arctic north there is an icy plain, the tundra. To the south of this there are huge forests, the home of brown bears. The countryside also takes in rolling farmland called steppes, deserts and high mountain ranges. Europe's longest river is the Volga, over 3,500 kilometres long, which flows into the Caspian Sea. To the east is Baikal, the deepest lake in the world.

Before 1991 all the countries on this map were part of one huge country called the Soviet Union. After 1991 many of the lands around the Soviet borders broke away to form separate countries. Over a hundred different peoples live in the region, beside the Russians themselves.

St Basil's Cathedral stands in Red Square, in Moscow.

In the days of the Soviet Union, big statues were put up showing people working hard for their country. These **farmers** are harvesting wheat. It is still an important crop today.

FINLAND

BARENTS SEA

Murmansk

Archangel

St Petersburg

BELARUS

Minsk

Moscow

UKRAINE

Kiev

Nizhniy Novgorod

Kazan

Chisinau

MOLDOVA

Don

Volga

Samara

URAL MOUNTAINS

Yekaterinb

Ural

BLACK SEA

GEORGIA
ARMENIA
AZERBAIJAN

Caspian Sea

KAZAKHSTAN

Aral Sea

Aqm

TURKMENISTAN

Bishke

IRAN

Ashgabat

Tashkent

Dushan

TAJIKISTA

One-third of **Armenians** still work on the land. They produce vegetables and fruit or raise sheep and cattle.

In the Middle Ages, Russian monks made beautiful **Bibles** like this one, and painted holy pictures called icons.

Fine **silk** is produced and woven into cloth in the Imeretia region of Georgia.

Wrangel I.

Franz Josef Land

Severnaya Zemlya

New Siberian Islands

ovaya Zemlya

KARA SEA

KAMCHATKA PENINSULA

EAST SIBERIAN UPLANDS

CENTRAL SIBERIAN PLATEAU

Lena

Yenisey

Yakutsk

SEA OF OKHOTSK

Sakhalin

RUSSIA

Ob

Angara

Amur

Khabarovsk

Sour cream

msk

Novosibirsk

Irkutsk

Lake Baykal

CHINA

Vladivostok

Blinis

Beetroot

CHINA

maty

YRGYZSTAN

Borscht is made from beetroots and served with sour cream and blinis.

Canada and Greenland

ARCTIC
OCEAN

Most Canadian towns are in the south, near the United States border, the Great Lakes or the St Lawrence River. The north is a wilderness, with frozen plains, vast forests, mountains and blue lakes. Winters are long and severe, but summers can be mild or warm. Most Canadians are English-speaking, descended from British settlers. A large number are French-speaking, especially in the province of Québec. There are also First Peoples, such as the Innu, Mohawk, Cree and Micmac. In Arctic Canada are the Inuit people, who traditionally live by hunting seals and polar bears.

Inuit people also live in Greenland, along with descendants of Danish settlers. This is the world's largest island. Its rocky land is covered in a thick sheet of Arctic ice.

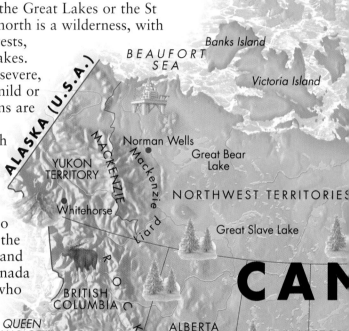

Banks Island

BEAUFORT
SEA

Victoria Island

ALASKA (U.S.A.)

Norman Wells

Great Bear
Lake

YUKON
TERRITORY

MACKENZIE

Mackenzie

NORTHWEST TERRITORIES

Whitehorse

Liard

Great Slave Lake

R
O
C
K
Y

BRITISH
COLUMBIA

CAN

ALBERTA

MANITOBA

QUEEN
CHARLOTTE
ISLANDS

SASKATCHEWAN

Calgary

Vancouver
Island

Vancouver

Regina

Winnipeg

UNITED STATES OF AMERICA

Maple trees grow colourful leaves in autumn. The maple leaf is a badge of Canada and is shown on the national flag.

Totem poles are still raised outside villages by the First Peoples of British Columbia. They are carved with birds and beasts and figures from myths, legends and family history.

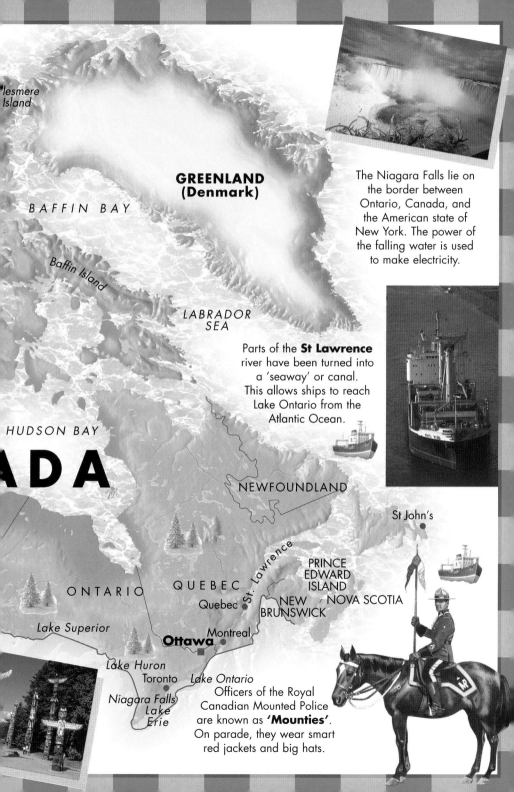

'lesmere
Island

GREENLAND
(Denmark)

BAFFIN BAY

Baffin Island

*LABRADOR
SEA*

HUDSON BAY

ADA

NEWFOUNDLAND

St John's

PRINCE
EDWARD
ISLAND

St. Lawrence

QUEBEC   NEW   NOVA SCOTIA
                BRUNSWICK
Quebec

ONTARIO

Lake Superior

Ottawa   Montreal

Lake Huron
Toronto   *Lake Ontario*

Niagara Falls
*Lake
Erie*

The Niagara Falls lie on
the border between
Ontario, Canada, and
the American state of
New York. The power of
the falling water is used
to make electricity.

Parts of the **St Lawrence**
river have been turned into
a 'seaway' or canal.
This allows ships to reach
Lake Ontario from the
Atlantic Ocean.

Officers of the Royal
Canadian Mounted Police
are known as **'Mounties'**.
On parade, they wear smart
red jackets and big hats.

The United States of America

The North American **raccoon** is a furry little creature with black patches on its eyes and a ringed tail. It comes out by night.

The United States of America (USA) stretch the whole way from the Atlantic Ocean to the Pacific. There are 50 states in all. They take in woodlands, whose leaves turn red and gold each autumn, and long ranges of hills such as the Appalachians. They include the Great Lakes and the rivers Mississippi and Missouri, which flow into the steamy Gulf of Mexico. There are wide open grasslands called prairies, which are given over to farming and cattle ranching. There is the great Rocky Mountain chain. There are the burning dry deserts of the southwest and the rainy, misty forests of Oregon and Washington State. Two American states are separated from the others. They are Alaska, stretching from Canada into the frozen Arctic, and Hawaii, a group of islands and volcanoes far out in the Pacific Ocean.

CANADA

Seattle
WASHINGTON
CASCADE RANGE
OREGON
MONTANA
IDAHO
Snake
Black Hills
WYOMING
Rapid C
Great Salt Lake
Rock Springs
Boulder
NEVADA
UTAH
Denve
San Francisco
GREAT BASIN
Grand Junction
COLORAD
Las Vegas
CALIFORNIA
Grand Canyon
NEW MEXICO
Los Angeles
Colorado
ARIZONA
Rio Grande
San Diego
Phoenix
Douglas
MEXICO

Rainbow Bridge is an arch of pink rock in the state of Utah. Over the ages, wind and water have worn it down into this strange shape.

The Roosevelt Dam stretches across the Salt River in Arizona. It was built in the early part of this century and irrigates rich farmland.

Huge heads have been carved from the rock at **Mount Rushmore**, in South Dakota. They show famous presidents of the USA.

Oranges, lemons and grapefruit are **citrus fruits**. They are grown in the far west, in California, and also in the southeastern state of Florida.

Lake Superior
MINNESOTA
Marquette
Lake Huron
WISCONSIN
MICHIGAN
Lake Michigan
Lake Erie
RTH KOTA
marck
SOUTH DAKOTA
rre
Mississippi
IOWA
Chicago
INDIANA
ILLINOIS
OHIO
Ohio
WEST VIRGINIA
Charleston
BRASKA
Miss
MAINE
VERMONT NEW HAMPSHIRE
MASSACHUSETTS
NEW YORK
Boston
Providence
RHODE IS.
CONNECTICUT
New York City
NEW JERSEY
PENNSYLVANIA
Philadelphia
DELAWARE
WASHINGTON D.C.
MARYLAND
Richmond
VIRGINIA

ANSA
MISSOURI
KENTUCKY
NORTH CAROLINA
TENNESSEE
APPALACHIAN MTS.
Chattanooga
SOUTH CAROLINA
KLAHOMA
ARKANSAS
Atlanta
MISSISSIPPI
Columbus
ALABAMA GEORGIA
EXAS
LOUISIANA
Houston
New Orleans
San Antonio
Orlando
FLORIDA
Miami
GULF OF MEXICO
Grande
Straits of Florida

American-style **hamburgers** and **doughnuts** are amongst the many fast foods that are now sold all over the world.

The USA has many big, bustling cities. In the west is San Francisco. It is a beautiful port beside the blue Pacific Ocean. Los Angeles is a huge city full of traffic. A part of it, called Hollywood, is where many famous films have been made. Chicago, on Lake Michigan, was where skyscrapers were first built, over a hundred years ago. Detroit, on Lake Erie, is where many American cars are made. And New York City, in the east, is the biggest city of them all. It is nicknamed the Big Apple. The capital of the country is Washington. This is the centre of government and is also where the US president lives, in the White House. It isn't in one of the states but in a special district called Columbia.

Many different peoples live in the USA today. Native Americans are descended from the very first people to settle in North America. They include peoples such as the Navajo, Apache and Cree. Many Americans are descended from European settlers.

ARCTIC OCEAN

BERING SEA

BROOK RANGE

CANADA

Bering Strait

ALASKA (U.S.A.)

St. Lawrence Island

Yukon

Mt McKinley 6194 m

Anchorage

GULF OF ALASKA

Juneau

PACIFIC OC

ALEUTIAN ISLANDS

The **World Trade Centre** has two tall towers. They rise up from the water's edge on the island of Manhattan. This is right at the centre of New York City, one of the largest and busiest cities in the world.

Rattlesnakes live in the hot, dry lands of Texas and the southwest. They are very dangerous. They rattle their tails as a warning before they bite you.

Dance and song make up a **traditional welcome** to the Hawaiian islands. Hawaii's links with the USA go back 100 years.

KAUAI

NIIHAU

OAHU

Honolulu

MOLOKAI

LANAI

MAUI

KAHOOLAWE

Hilo

HAWAII

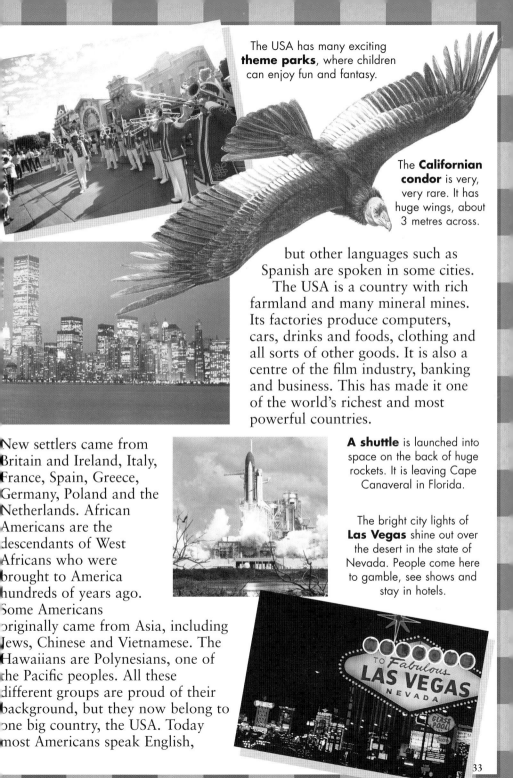

The USA has many exciting **theme parks**, where children can enjoy fun and fantasy.

The **Californian condor** is very, very rare. It has huge wings, about 3 metres across.

but other languages such as Spanish are spoken in some cities. The USA is a country with rich farmland and many mineral mines. Its factories produce computers, cars, drinks and foods, clothing and all sorts of other goods. It is also a centre of the film industry, banking and business. This has made it one of the world's richest and most powerful countries.

New settlers came from Britain and Ireland, Italy, France, Spain, Greece, Germany, Poland and the Netherlands. African Americans are the descendants of West Africans who were brought to America hundreds of years ago. Some Americans originally came from Asia, including Jews, Chinese and Vietnamese. The Hawaiians are Polynesians, one of the Pacific peoples. All these different groups are proud of their background, but they now belong to one big country, the USA. Today most Americans speak English,

A shuttle is launched into space on the back of huge rockets. It is leaving Cape Canaveral in Florida.

The bright city lights of **Las Vegas** shine out over the desert in the state of Nevada. People come here to gamble, see shows and stay in hotels.

TO Fabulous
LAS VEGAS
NEVADA

33

Mexico, Central America and the Caribbean

Guacamole

Chillies

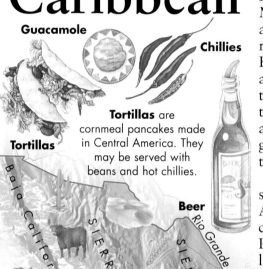

Tortillas are cornmeal pancakes made in Central America. They may be served with beans and hot chillies.

Tortillas

Beer

Mexico lies between the Gulf of Mexico and the Pacific Ocean. It is a land of hot deserts, mountain ranges, forests and sandy beaches. Earthquakes are common and there are volcanoes too. Mexico City is the country's capital. Once it was the chief city of the Aztec people and called Tenochtitlán. Many great civilizations were started in the region long ago.

To the south of Mexico are the seven small countries of Central America. Panama is crossed by a canal, which links the Atlantic and Pacific Oceans. Spanish is the main language of the region. Many of its

Baja California

SIERRA MADRE

SIERRA MADRE

Río Grande

Matamoros

Culiacán   Monterrey

Havana

CU

GULF OF MEXICO

Guadalajara   León

Cancún

Cayman Islands (U.

Mexico City Veracruz

MEXICO

Coatzacoalcas

Belmopan

BELIZE

Acapulco

GUATEMALA   HONDURAS

PACIFIC OCEAN

Guatemala City Tegucigalpa

These Native American women from **Guatemala** wear colourful clothes they have woven by hand. Each village has its own patterns and styles.

San Salvador
EL SALVADOR

NICARAGU

Managua

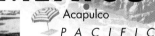

San José   Pana

COSTA RICA

PANA

peoples are descended from the Spanish soldiers who invaded the Americas nearly 500 years ago. Others are descended from Native Americans. Central American crops include maize and bananas.

The Caribbean Sea lies to the east of Central America. It has thousands of islands, the largest of which is Cuba. Caribbean peoples include many whose ancestors came from West Africa. There are also some Caribbeans of Native American, Spanish, French, British, Dutch and Asian descent. The islands have a warm, tropical climate in which sugarcane and bananas grow well. Hurricanes are common in the later summer and autumn. The islands are famous for their carnivals.

Brilliantly coloured **humming birds** hover as they sip nectar from flowers. They are found in both Central America and the Caribbean.

Warm blue seas, fine beaches and watersports attract millions of tourists to the Caribbean islands each year. This is **Barbados**.

How would you like to dive off this cliff into the sea? This is one of the sights to be seen at **Acapulco**, in Mexico.

AHAMAS

Turks & Caicos Islands (U.K.)

Virgin Is. (U.K. & U.S.)

Puerto Rico (U.S.)

HAITI

DOMINICAN REPUBLIC

AMAICA

C A R I B B E A N S E A

ANTIGUA & BARBUDA

ST. KITTS & NEVIS

Montserrat (U.K.)

Guadeloupe (FR.)

DOMINICA

Martinique (FR.)

ST. LUCIA

ST. VINCENT & THE GRENADINES

BARBADOS

GRENADA

TRINIDAD & TOBAGO

Mexico and parts of Central America have many ancient ruins and statues, like this **warrior** carved from stone. They date back to the ancient civilizations that once grew up here.

Old churches and buildings, like this one in **Costa Rica**, remind us that this region was once ruled by Spain.

35

The Northern Andes

South America is joined to Central America by a narrow strip of land. To the south, the Andes mountains run all the way down the continent. Their high, snowy peaks divide the hot lands along the coast from the rainforests and great rivers of the east.

Colombia is a beautiful country, which lies across three bands of the Andes range. The rocks are mined for gold and precious green stones called emeralds. Ecuador is named after the Spanish word for Equator. Bananas and sugarcane grow in the warm climate here, and coffee too on the slopes of hills. In Peru, farmers work high in the mountains, growing potatoes, maize and a grain called quinoa. Along the coast fishermen catch tuna and sardines. Bolivia has great forests and tin mines.

About 500 years ago, the Inca people ruled a huge empire in the Andes. It was conquered by Spanish soldiers. Many peoples of the region are descended from Native American peoples and from the Spanish.

This boat is made of reeds, by the **Aymara people.** They live around Lake Titicaca, which is on the border between Peru and Bolivia.

The green turtle lives in the sea along the coasts of Peru, Ecuador and Colombia. It breeds on lonely, sandy beaches and is becoming very rare.

CARIBBEAN SEA

PANAMA

VENEZUELA

Bogota

COLOMBIA

ECUADOR

Quito

Amazon

Iquitos

S

PERÚ

BOLIVIA

PARAGUAY

CHILE

N

Ucayali

Lima

Nazca

PACIFIC OCEAN

Lake Titicaca

La Paz

Lake Poopó

Sucre

pan-pipes

maracas

Andean musicians play the rondador or pan-pipes, rattles called maracas, guitars and drums.

This peak towers above the rocks of the **Andes**. It is covered in snow, even though it is near the Equator, in Ecuador. It is called Cotopaxi and is the world's highest active volcano.

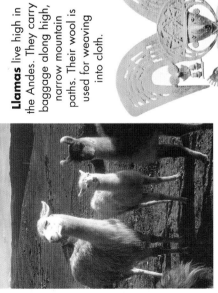

Llamas live high in the Andes. They carry baggage along high, narrow mountain paths. Their wool is used for weaving into cloth.

This mother and baby belong to the **Quechua people**. They live near the old Inca capital of Cuzco, in Peru. Most Quechua live in mountain villages and work as farmers. They grow potatoes and maize, and raise sheep and llamas.

The ancient peoples of Colombia made many beautiful things from **gold** and precious stones. They used knives like these for their religious ceremonies.

Brazil and its Neighbours

Brazil is the biggest country in South America. It is a hot country with grassland, swamps and dry bush. A large area is covered in rainforest. This is the home of monkeys, brightly coloured parrots and gigantic snakes called anacondas. One of the world's two longest rivers, the Amazon, flows through the forest to the Atlantic Ocean.

On the coast there are many big cities. Some city dwellers are rich, but many are very poor.

Venezuela is on the Caribbean coast. It is crossed by another great river called the Orinoco.

A large sea inlet called Lake Maracaibo is the centre of Venezuela's oil industry. Three other small countries, called Guyana, Surinam and French Guiana, lie on the tropical north coast. They produce sugarcane, rice, chilli peppers and fruits.

This part of South America is home to many different Native American peoples, as well as people descended from Africans and Europeans. The region was once ruled by Portugal, Spain, France, Britain and the Netherlands.

The **Iguaçu Falls** lie on the border between Brazil and Argentina. The river thunders over hundreds of waterfalls.

VENEZUELA
Caracas
Orinoco
COLOMBIA
PERU

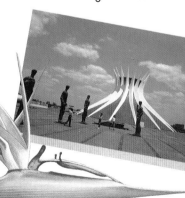

This cathedral is in **Brasília**, the capital of Brazil. This modern city was specially built inland, to the south of the great forests.

There are many different kinds of **poison-arrow frog** in South America. Their deadly poison is smeared on arrows and darts by Native American hunters.

This beautiful tropical plant is called the **bird-of-paradise flower**.

TRINIDAD & TOBAGO

Angel Falls

Georgetown

GUYANA

Paramaribo

Cayenne

SURINAM

FRENCH GUIANA

G U I A N A

legro

A m a z o n

Manaus

Santarém

In the southeast of **Venezuela** there are sheer, flat-topped mountains called tepuis. They rise from beautiful lakes and green tropical forests.

Teresina

Fortaleza

BRAZIL

uaporé

BOLIVIA

Salvador

■ **Brasília**

P a r a n á

Belo Horizonte

São Paulo

Rio de Janeiro

Many tropical trees grow in Brazil. One produces seeds called **brazil nuts**. They make delicious snacks.

The **puma** is a big, fierce cat. In North America it is called the cougar or mountain lion.

ARGENTINA

Uruguay

URUGUAY

A big **statue of Jesus** looks out over the city of Rio de Janeiro, in Brazil. It is on a high mountain called the Sugarloaf.

Argentina and its Neighbours

Southern South America is a big triangle of land. The pointed end stretches south towards Antarctica. It breaks up into islands around Tierra del Fuego. Gales whip up huge waves around the southern tip, which is called Cape Horn. As you travel north, you come to the dry, windy valleys of Patagonia, the high Andes mountains, the rich grassland of the Pampas and the hot, damp Gran Chaco region.

Argentina is a big country, which raises beef cattle and sheep. It borders the Atlantic Ocean. Far offshore are the remote Falkland or Malvinas islands. Uruguay and Paraguay are two small countries to the north, which also raise cattle. Chile, to the west of the Andes, is a long, narrow land. It borders the Pacific Ocean. It has large areas of desert, where it hardly ever rains. It also has warm farmland, where grapes can be grown.

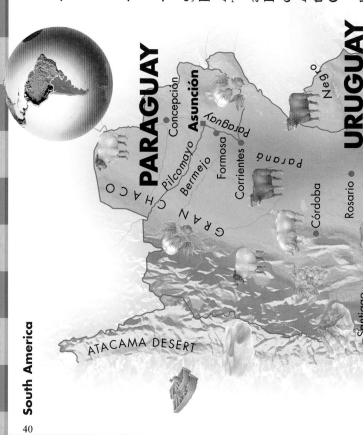

PARAGUAY

Concepción

Asunción

Paraguay

Pilcomayo

Bermejo

Formosa

Corrientes

G R A N   C H A C O

Córdoba

Paraná

Rosario

Negro

URUGUAY   ■ Montevideo

Buenos Aires

P A M P A S

Santiago

ATACAMA DESERT

CHILE

Concepción

ARGENTINA

The snow-capped volcano of **Villarrica** rises above a milder landscape near Pucón, in Chile.

Tomatoes were first grown in South America, on the slopes of the Andes mountains. Today they are grown all over the world.

The **gauchos** are the cowboys of the Pampas grasslands in Argentina. They are skilled at riding horses and roping cattle. They used to be famous for their wild adventures.

Ushuaia is a port in **Tierra del Fuego**, in the far south of Argentina. The people who live there raise sheep and go fishing.

FALKLAND/MALVINAS ISLANDS

• Stanley

Cape Horn

Tierra del Fuego

The **rhea** is a large South American bird that can grow to 1.5 m tall. It cannot fly and lives on the Pampas.

PACIFIC OCEAN

PATAGONIA

Montt

41

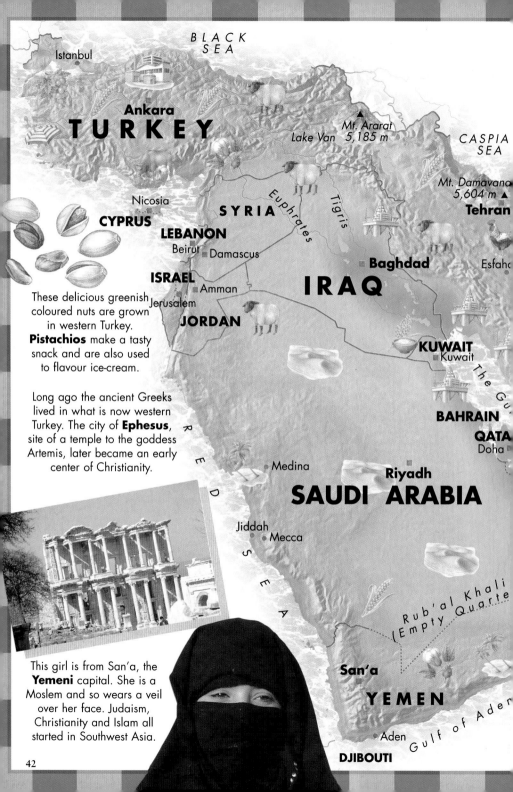

B L A C K
S E A

Istanbul

Ankara

T U R K E Y

Mt. Ararat
5,185 m

Lake Van

C A S P I A
S E A

Mt. Damavana
5,604 m ▲

Tehran

Nicosia

S Y R I A

Euphrates

Tigris

CYPRUS

LEBANON

Beirut • Damascus

ISRAEL

Amman

Jerusalem

Baghdad

IRAQ

Esfaho

These delicious greenish
coloured nuts are grown
in western Turkey.
Pistachios make a tasty
snack and are also used
to flavour ice-cream.

JORDAN

KUWAIT
Kuwait

The Gu

Long ago the ancient Greeks
lived in what is now western
Turkey. The city of **Ephesus**,
site of a temple to the goddess
Artemis, later became an early
center of Christianity.

BAHRAIN

QATA
Doha

Medina

Riyadh

SAUDI ARABIA

R
E
D

Jiddah

S

Mecca

E

A

Rub'al Khali
(Empty Quarte

This girl is from San'a, the
Yemeni capital. She is a
Moslem and so wears a veil
over her face. Judaism,
Christianity and Islam all
started in Southwest Asia.

San'a

Y E M E N

Aden •

Gulf of Aden

DJIBOUTI

42

Southwest Asia

This region of Asia is often called the Near East or the Middle East. Its western parts border the Mediterranean Sea. These have a gentle, warm climate, which makes it possible to grow fruits such as oranges and lemons. The Arabian peninsula is the land surrounded by the Red Sea, the Indian Ocean and the Persian Gulf. It is occupied by Jordan, Israel, Saudi Arabia and the small countries of Yemen, Oman, United Arab Emirates (UAE), Qatar, Bahrain and Kuwait. This a land of hot, sandy deserts. Little can grow here, but it is rich in oil and natural gas.

Eastern Syria and Iraq are also desert regions, but these are crossed by the Rivers Tigris and Euphrates. It was here that the world's first farmers founded towns and cities thousands of years ago. Eastern Turkey and northern Iran include mountains, windswept plains and rolling grasslands, which are very cold in winter. Iran also has ranges of mountains and deserts.

Mashhad

IRAN

Abu Dhabi

Gulf of Oman

Muscat

UNITED ARAB EMIRATES

OMAN

These towers in **Kuwait** are used to take the salt out of sea water, so that it can be drunk or used on the land.

Beautiful **pearls** form in oysters in the warm seas of Southwest Asia. They are very valuable.

This camel rider is one of the **Bedouin**, a nomadic people of the region. Camels are the ideal transport for desert areas.

Socotra (YEMEN)

43

India and its Neighbours

This mass of land is so big that it is sometimes called the Indian subcontinent, or simply the subcontinent. It is separated from Central Asia by the world's biggest mountains, which are in the Himalaya and Karakoram ranges. These climb to 8,848 metres above sea level at Mount Everest. Snowy peaks stretch all the way from eastern Afghanistan, through northern Pakistan and India to Nepal and Bhutan.

To the south are the wide, dusty plains of India, crossed by the Ganges. In Bangladesh, this river splits into many channels before flowing into the Bay of Bengal. India is a country of deserts, forested hills, small villages and large bustling cities. The climate is mostly tropical and very hot, with monsoon winds bringing heavy summer rainstorms. In the far south is the tropical island nation of Sri Lanka. The region produces wheat, tea, sugarcane, rice, jute and cotton. It includes the sites of ancient civilizations and places which are holy to Hindus, Buddhists, Sikhs and Moslems.

Mount Everest is the highest mountain on Earth. It lies on the border between Nepal and Tibet, in the Himalaya range.

Colourful, sparkling costumes are worn by these **Indian dancers**. India is famous for its richly coloured silks and cottons and its silver jewellery.

AFGHANISTAN

Kabul

Khyber Pass

Islamabad

Lahore

PAKISTAN

Indus

NEPAL

Delhi ▪ **New Delhi**

HIMALAYAS

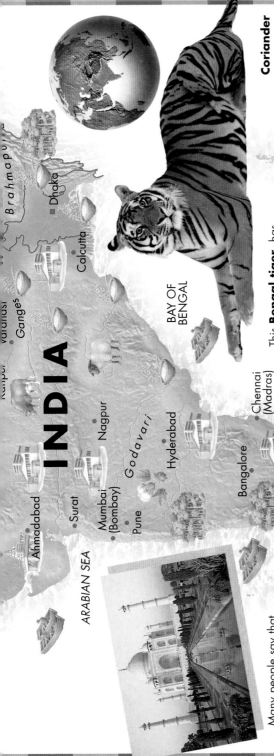

Coriander

Ground turmeric

Andaman & Nicobar Is. (India)

Ginger

Indian food includes delicious curries, chutneys, rice and vegetable dishes. They are cooked with different **kinds of spice.**

This **Bengal tiger** has become very rare. It is protected in special reserves in India, Bangladesh and Nepal.

Brahmaputra

Dhaka

Calcutta

Varanasi

Ganges

INDIA

Kanpur

Nagpur

Godavari

Hyderabad

BAY OF BENGAL

Chennai (Madras)

Bangalore

Ahmadabad

Surat

Mumbai (Bombay)

Pune

ARABIAN SEA

SRI LANKA

Colombo

Galle

INDIAN OCEAN

A woman picks **tea** in the green hills of Sri Lanka. This small island nation to the south of India is the biggest exporter of tea in the world.

MALDIVES

Many people say that the **Taj Mahal,** a marble tomb, is the most beautiful building in the world. It was built near Agra in India by a Moslem emperor called Shah Jahan, who ruled from 1627 to 1666.

45

China and its Neighbours

China covers an area about the size of western Europe. It is ringed by high mountains, empty deserts and tropical seas where fierce storms called typhoons are common.

Most people live in the fertile eastern part of the country, which is crossed by great rivers such as the Huang He and the Chang Jiang. More people live in China than in any other country in the world. Chinese farmers grow rice, tea, wheat and maize. China is the centre of a very ancient civilization and was famous in history for its pottery and fine silk.

The Mongols live in a northern part of China and also in the rolling grasslands and deserts of Mongolia itself. The Koreans live to the northeast, on a peninsula containing North and South Korea.

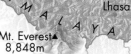

KAZAKHSTAN

MONGOLIA

Ürümqi

TAKLIMAKAN DESERT

CHINA

INDIA

PLATEAU OF TIBET

HIMALAYA

Lhasa

Salw

Mt. Everest▲ 8,848m

Qin Shi Huangdi was the first emperor of China. When he died in 210BC his tomb was surrounded by a **buried army**. This was made up of thousands of life-sized soldiers, made of clay.

Traditional wooden sailing boats called **junks** may still be seen amongst the more modern ships around the coasts of China.

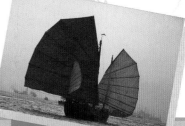

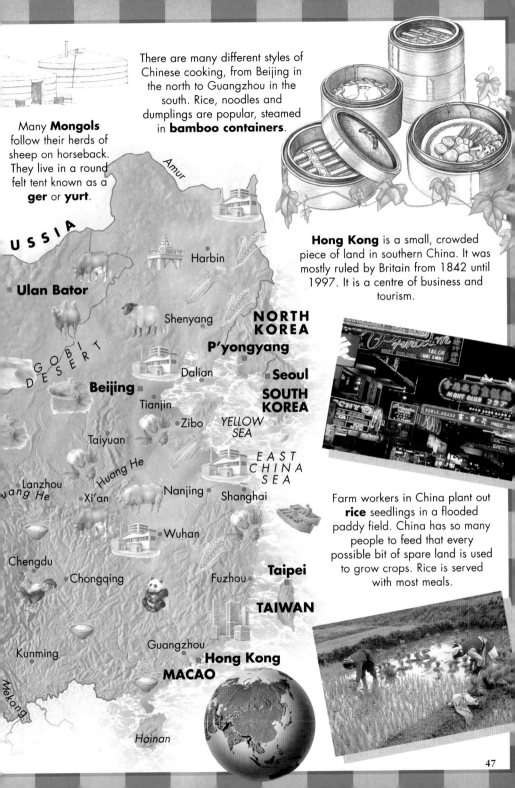

There are many different styles of Chinese cooking, from Beijing in the north to Guangzhou in the south. Rice, noodles and dumplings are popular, steamed in **bamboo containers**.

Many **Mongols** follow their herds of sheep on horseback. They live in a round felt tent known as a **ger** or **yurt**.

Hong Kong is a small, crowded piece of land in southern China. It was mostly ruled by Britain from 1842 until 1997. It is a centre of business and tourism.

Farm workers in China plant out **rice** seedlings in a flooded paddy field. China has so many people to feed that every possible bit of spare land is used to grow crops. Rice is served with most meals.

U S S I A

Amur

Ulan Bator

GOBI DESERT

Harbin

Shenyang

NORTH KOREA

P'yongyang

Dalian

Beijing

Tianjin

Taiyuan

Zibo

Seoul

SOUTH KOREA

YELLOW SEA

Lanzhou

Huang He

ang He

Xi'an

Nanjing

EAST CHINA SEA

Shanghai

Chengdu

Wuhan

Chongqing

Fuzhou

Taipei

TAIWAN

Kunming

Guangzhou

Hong Kong

MACAO

Mekong

Hainan

Japan

Kuril Is.
(Russia)

HOKKAIDO

▲ Asahi Mt.
2,290 m

Sapporo

Kitak

The Japanese capital is **Tokyo**. It is a centre of business and industry and merges with another great city, the port of Yokohama. It has suffered in the past from severe earthquakes.

The high-speed **Bullet Train** has become a symbol of modern Japan. Japan's islands are linked by some of the world's longest and most modern bridges and tunnels.

Thousands of small islands lie to the east of China on the edge of the Pacific Ocean. They make up a country called Japan. There are four main islands – Hokkaido, Honshu, Shikoku and Kyushu. These are mostly very mountainous, so the big cities have spread along the strips of flat land around the coast. This is where most of the good farmland is sited, too. Japan produces rice and tea, and has a large fishing fleet. The north of the country is cold and snowy in winter, but the south has a warm, tropical climate.

Japan has very few resources such as oil or coal. Even so, it is a very modern country which has many big businesses and produces cars and electrical goods. At the same time Japan is an ancient country, with many traditional customs and ceremonies. You can still see beautiful Buddhist temples and castles too, dating back to the Middle Ages. Japan has long been famous for its beautiful art, architecture and pottery. Japanese artists carry on these traditions in modern dance, the cinema and even in computer games.

JAPAN

The slopes of **Mount Fuji** are covered in snow. Japanese artists have painted this beautiful volcano many times.

Traditional dress is still worn in Japan on many special occasions. This woman wears sandals and a silk gown called a kimono.

Sumo wrestlers weigh in at about 135 kilograms. Their aim is to topple their opponent or throw them out of the ring. The match starts with long ceremonies, but the action is normally over very quickly.

Favourite Japanese foods

include rice, fish, prawns, seaweed, pork, bean curd and noodles. These are traditionally eaten with chopsticks.

Sendai

Mito

HONSHU **Tokyo**

Yokohama

Mt. Fuji 3,776 m

PACIFIC OCEAN

Nagoya

Kyoto

Kobe Osaka

Kii Channel

SHIKOKU

Hiroshima

Kitakyushu

Fukuoka

KYUSHU

49

Southeast Asia

The southeast of the Asian continent borders India and China. It is a land of flooded ricefields, forests, remote hill country and great rivers, such as the Irrawaddy and the Mekong. This region has beautiful Buddhist temples and ruins left behind by ancient civilizations. Sadly, it has also seen terrible wars in the last 50 years, while in some areas the traditional way of life has been completely changed by tourism or, in the cities of Singapore or Kuala Lumpur, by big business.

The mainland states include Myanmar, Thailand, Cambodia, Laos and Vietnam. Malaysia takes up part of the mainland but also most of the forested, tropical island of Borneo. The small state of Brunei is in the north of Borneo. The south of the region is occupied by the long chains of islands which make up Indonesia. In the far east, bordering the Pacific Ocean are the Philippines.

INDIA

MYANMAR (BURMA) CHINA

Hano

Yangon (Rangoon) **LAOS** Vientiane

THAILAND

Bangkok

CAMBODI

Phnom Penh

Ho Chi Minh Ci'

Gulf of Thailand

M A L

Medan Strait of Malacca Kuala Lump

Sumatra **SINGAPO**

Jakart

People of both Indian and Chinese descent live in the city of **Singapore** and their styles of cooking have mingled – deliciously!

This ornate stone demon guards the royal palace in **Bangkok**, capital of Thailand.

The **orang-utan** lives in the rainforests of Borneo and Sumatra. Throughout Southeast Asia forests are threatened by logging, clearance and fires.

IETNAM

A boat is anchored by the banks of the Hue river, in northeastern **Vietnam**. Cone-shaped straw hats protect the wearer from tropical sun and monsoon rains.

While most Indonesians are Moslems, the **Balinese** are Hindus. The island of Bali has many beautiful old temples and palaces, where dances like this can be seen.

Luzon

■ Manila

PHILIPPINES

SULU SEA

Mindanao

Bandar Seri Begawan

S I A **BRUNEI**

CELEBES SEA

BORNEO

Moluccas

Sulawesi

I N D O N E S I A

NEW GUINEA

A V A *SEA*

BANDA SEA

va Surabaya *FLORES SEA*

Lombok
Bali *Sumba*

Timor

Singapore is a tiny independent country. Most of it is taken up by the city of Singapore, an international centre of business and trade.

Meet the **komodo dragon**, the world's biggest lizard. It lives only on Komodo and a few neighbouring islands in Indonesia.

North and West Africa

The Mediterranean coast has a pleasant, warm climate. To the south, beyond the Atlas mountains, is the world's largest desert, the Sahara. Its burning hot sands and rocks stretch all the way from Mauritania to Egypt. The River Nile, the world's longest river, meets the sea in Egypt after a long journey northwards across Sudan. It rises in the mountains of Central Africa and Ethiopia.

The countries bordering the southern edge of the Sahara make up the Sahel. This is a dry, dusty region where thin grass is grazed by cattle and goats. Nearer the coast, on the Gulf of Guinea, there is fertile farmland, forest and the oil-rich lands around the River Niger. West Africa produces peanuts, cocoa, palm oil and cotton.

Peoples of the north include Berbers and Arabs. The many different peoples living to the south of the Sahara are mostly Black Africans. Religions of the region include Islam, Christianity and spirit religions.

Strait of Gibral
Madeira Casablanca Rabat
MOROCCO ATLAS MTS
CANARY
ISLANDS
ALGER
**Western
Sahara** S A
Cape
Blanc
MAURITANIA
Nouakchott
MALI
Timbuktu
Dakar
SENEGAL Niger
Banjul **GAMBIA**
Bissau
Bamako Nia
Ouagadougou
GUINEA- GUINEA
BISSAU Conakry
BURKINA FA
Freetown **SIERRA
LEONE**
**IVORY
COAST** **GHANA** **TOGO**
Monrovia
LIBERIA Yamoussoukro Lomé Lo
Abidjan Accra N

This grumpy-looking camel is looking out over the **Pyramids**, the royal burial sites of ancient Egypt. Africa's first great civilization grew up in Egypt about 5,000 years ago.

Tutankhamun died in 1327BC. He was ruler, or pharaoh, of ancient Egypt and was buried with all sorts of rich treasures.

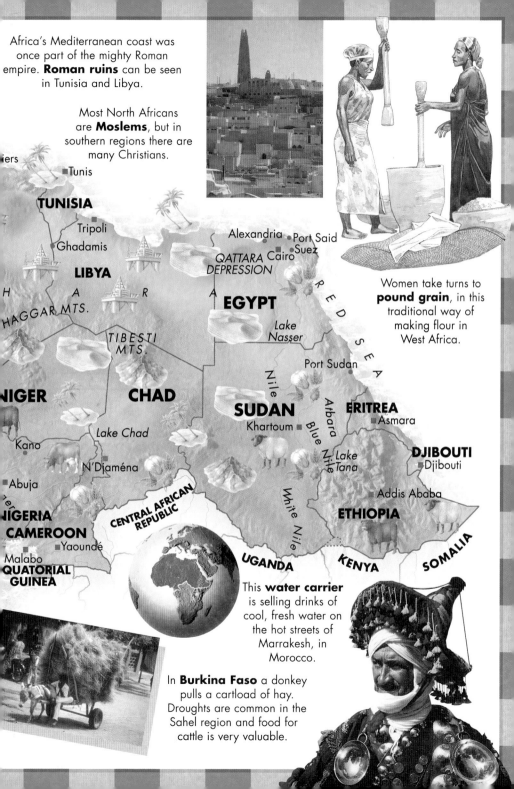

Africa's Mediterranean coast was once part of the mighty Roman empire. **Roman ruins** can be seen in Tunisia and Libya.

Most North Africans are **Moslems**, but in southern regions there are many Christians.

iers

■Tunis

TUNISIA

Tripoli

Ghadamis

LIBYA

Alexandria   Port Said
Suez
Cairo
*QATTARA
DEPRESSION*

H A G G A R

HAGGAR MTS.

*TIBESTI
MTS.*

EGYPT

*Lake
Nasser*

Women take turns to **pound grain**, in this traditional way of making flour in West Africa.

Port Sudan

NIGER

CHAD

Lake Chad

Kano

N'Djaména

■Abuja

NIGERIA

CAMEROON

Yaoundé

Malabo

**QUATORIAL
GUINEA**

Nile

SUDAN

Khartoum

Atbara

Blue Nile

*Lake
Tana*

ERITREA

Asmara

DJIBOUTI

■Djibouti

Addis Ababa

ETHIOPIA

**CENTRAL AFRICAN
REPUBLIC**

White Nile

UGANDA

KENYA

SOMALIA

This **water carrier** is selling drinks of cool, fresh water on the hot streets of Marrakesh, in Morocco.

In **Burkina Faso** a donkey pulls a cartload of hay. Droughts are common in the Sahel region and food for cattle is very valuable.

Central, Eastern and Southern Africa

Central Africa is a land of rainforests, crossed by the River Congo. To the south are the Kalahari and Namib deserts, and the mountains and grasslands of South Africa. The east of the continent is divided by the Great Rift Valley, a network of deep cracks in the Earth's surface. It is fringed by volcanoes and in places has filled with water to form long lakes. East Africa includes rich farmland, which produces tobacco, fruit and vegetables. There are wide grassy plains dotted with thorny trees, grazed by great herds of wild animals including zebra, giraffe and many types of antelope. The continent is bordered by the Atlantic to the west and by the Indian Ocean to the east. Madagascar is Africa's largest island.

The **Masai people** live in southern Kenya and northern Tanzania. Many of them herd cattle.

SÃO TOMÉ & PRÍNCIPE
Libreville
Boz
REP. C
CONG
GABON
Brazzav
Kinshe
Cabinda (ANGOLA)
Luanda
A N

Vast herds of wild animals still roam eastern and southern Africa. They include lion, antelope, **elephant** and rhinoceros.

NAMIB DESERT
Windho

Wind shapes the shifiting sands of the **Namib desert** in southwestern Africa. This harsh, dry region borders the Atlantic coast for 1,280 kilometres.

Sorghum is a grain crop much like corn which thrives in the hot and dry conditions of Zimbabwe.

Cape T
Cape
Good I

The **Zulus** are the largest group of peoples living in South Africa. Many different peoples live in the region, each with their own language and traditions.

The River Zambezi forms **Victoria Falls,** a huge waterfall, between Zambia and Zimbabwe. Its local name is Mose-la-Tunya, the 'smoke that thunders'.

SOMALIA

CENTRAL AFRICAN REPUBLIC
Bangassou
gui
ongo
Uele
UGANDA
Kampala
RWANDA Lake
Kigali Victoria

DEMOCRATIC REP. OF CONGO
Kananga
Sankuru
Kasai

KENYA
Mogadishu
Nairobi

▲ Kilimanjaro
5,895 m
Dodoma

BURUNDI
Lake
Tanganyika

TANZANIA

Lake Malawi
(Nyasa)

MALAWI
Lilongwe

ZAMBIA
Lusaka
Zambezi
Blantyre
Harare

MOZAMBIQUE

Moçambique

INDIAN OCEAN

SEYCHELLES

COMOROS

Mozambique Channel

ZIMBABWE

NAMIBIA

BOTSWANA
Gaborone
KALAHARI DESERT
Pretoria Maputo
Mbabane
SWAZILAND
Maseru

SOUTH AFRICA
LESOTHO

Limpopo

Antananarivo

MADAGASCAR

MAURITIUS

This animal is a ring-tailed **lemur**. Lemurs are only found on the island of Madagascar. They live in forest and dry scrub land, where they eat fruit and insects.

55

Australia

The centre of Australia is an empty wilderness of desert, rocks and scrub. It is bordered by grasslands, tropical forests and creeks. In the east are the mountains of the Great Dividing Range. The chief rivers are the Murray and the Darling, in the southeast. The remote country regions of Australia are known as the 'outback'. They are grazed by huge herds of sheep and cattle, and in places are worked by mining companies.

Most Australians live in the big cities around the coast, such as Brisbane, Sydney, Melbourne, Adelaide and Perth. Across Bass Strait is the island of Tasmania, which has a cooler climate.

Today's Australians include the first inhabitants of the land, the Aborigines, as well as the descendants of British people who seized their lands about 200 years ago. There are also many people from other European countries and from Asia.

Sydney Opera House rises from Sydney Harbour like a giant sailing ship.

A **giant clam** lies in the tropical waters of this 2,000 kilometre-long bank of coral.

GREA
SAND
DESE

GIBS(
DESE

**WESTERN
AUSTRALIA**

GREA
VICTO
DESE

Perth

Archipelago of
Recherche

Through the surf **rowers** break white water during a beach contest. Australia is famous for its surf.

The **kookaburra** is a common Australian bird. It has a loud cackling call which gives it the nickname of the laughing jackass.

Surfers' Paradise is one of many resorts built along the eastern coast of Australia. Sunshine and surf attract many visitors.

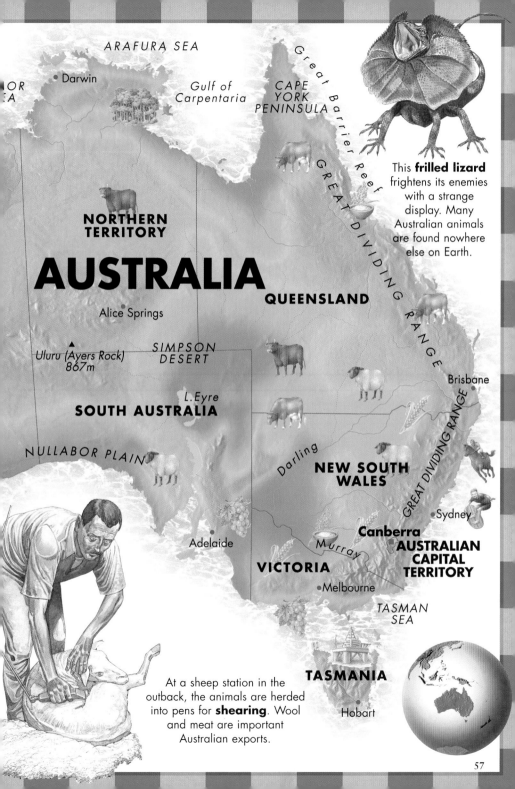

ARAFURA SEA

Darwin

Gulf of
Carpentaria

CAPE
YORK
PENINSULA

This **frilled lizard** frightens its enemies with a strange display. Many Australian animals are found nowhere else on Earth.

**NORTHERN
TERRITORY**

AUSTRALIA

Alice Springs

QUEENSLAND

▲ Uluru (Ayers Rock)
867m

SIMPSON
DESERT

L.Eyre

SOUTH AUSTRALIA

Brisbane

NULLABOR PLAIN

Darling

**NEW SOUTH
WALES**

Adelaide

GREAT DIVIDING RANGE

Sydney

Murray

Canberra
**AUSTRALIAN
CAPITAL
TERRITORY**

VICTORIA

Melbourne

TASMAN
SEA

At a sheep station in the outback, the animals are herded into pens for **shearing**. Wool and meat are important Australian exports.

TASMANIA

Hobart

57

New Zealand and the Pacific

If you sail eastwards from Australia, you reach a group of islands about 1,600 kilometres out into the Pacific Ocean. They make up a country called New Zealand. There are two main islands, North and South. They include high mountains and glaciers, hot springs, gushing spouts called geysers and grassy plains. The Maori people were the first people to settle these islands, followed after the 1800s by Europeans, especially the British. New Zealand raises sheep and exports dairy products, fruit and meat.

The Pacific is the world's biggest ocean stretching all the way to the Americas. It is dotted with small islands, and these are home to three main groups of people – the Polynesians (who include the Maoris), the Micronesians and the Melanesians. They live by fishing, growing crops such as coconuts and yams, by mining and by tourism.

Yellow Sea

East China Sea

SOUTH CHINA SEA

Philippine Sea

Northern Marian Islands (USA)

Guam

Federated States of Micronesia

Palau

Celebes Sea

Papua New Guinea

Solc Isl

Cora Sea

Papua New Guinea is made up of many islands. Some small islands are surrounded by shallow reefs.

This is a market in **Vanuatu,** a Pacific nation made up of 80 islands. They produce cocoa, dried coconut and bananas.

The **Kiwi** is a flightless bird which comes out by night to search for insects on the forest floor. It is the national emblem of New Zealand.

This **Karawari woman** from Papua New Guinea has painted her face for a traditional tribal gathering.

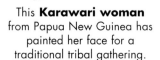

BERING SEA

Giant tortoises live on the Galapagos Islands. In fact the islands' name means 'tortoises' in Spanish. These Pacific Islands are governed by the South American country of Ecuador.

N O R T H
P A C I F I C
O C E A N

South Island, New Zealand, has snowfields, glaciers and **high mountains**. Mount Cook reaches 3,764 metres above sea level.

Midway
Island (USA)

'ake Island
(USA)   Hawaii (USA)

Marshall
Islands

The brown nut of the **coconut**, with its white centre, is found inside a large green fruit. Coconuts are a valuable Pacific island export.

Galapagos
(Ecuador)

uru   Kiribati

Tuvalu

nuat   Samoa   American
    Fiji   Samoa   French
                                    Polynesia

New   Tonga   Cook Islands
edonia   (New   Auckland
rance)   Zealand)
                                    Hamilton

                                    Rotorua
                                    L. Taupo
                                    Ruapehu   Napier
                                    2,797m   Hastings

Huge stone heads were carved by Polynesian settlers on **Easter Island**, about 1,000 years ago.

**NEW
:ALAND**

Kaibola canoes are the traditional means of transport of the Pacific Islands. This crew is from Papua New Guinea.

Palmerston North

Wellington

Mt.Cook
3,764m
            Christchurch

Clutha   Dunedin

Invercargill

Stewart Island

This fine **wooden carving** was placed above the door of a Moari building.

Traditionally, **Maoris** wore cloaks and tattooed their faces. Maoris today retain many customs.

59

Polar Lands

The northern part of the globe is called the Arctic. It takes in the northern parts of North America, Europe and Asia. These are lands of ice and snow and deep-frozen treeless soil, called tundra. They surround the Arctic Ocean, of which large areas are permanently capped in thick ice. At the centre of this ice cap is the northernmost point on Earth, the North Pole.

Peoples of the Arctic include the Inuit of Greenland and Canada, the Saami of Scandinavia and the many peoples from the north of the Russian Federation, such as the Chukchi, Yupigyts, Evenks and Samoyeds. Some live by hunting and fishing, some by herding reindeer and some in more recent Arctic industries, such as oil and mining. The Arctic Ocean supports fish, whales, walrus and seals.

The **Inuit people** live in Canada and Greenland. Traditionally their hunters made overnight camps out of blocks of frozen snow. These were shaped into domes.

BERING SEA

ALASKA (USA)

Mackenzie

CANADA

Victoria Island

New Siberian Islands

Lena

ARCTIC OCEAN

North Magnetic Pole

★ North Pole

Yenis

Ellesmere Island

Franz Josef Land

KARA SEA

Novaya Zemlya

Ob

GREENLAND (DENMARK)

Svalbard (Norway)

Murmansk

Archangel

ICELAND

Polar bears hunt seals on the ice.

The **Snowy owl** lives in Arctic regions.

Teams of dogs known as huskies, pull sleds across the snow in Antarctica.

The southernmost point on the globe is called the South Pole. It is surrounded by Antarctica, the coldest and windiest land on Earth. This is a land of mountains and dazzling white icefields, split by deep cracks called crevasses. Large areas of frozen sea surround the land. Massive slabs of ice break off in spring to form icebergs. No people have ever settled in Antarctica, but there are scientific bases. Some countries claim parts of Antarctica and there may be rich minerals in the rocks deep beneath the ice. However, many people think that Antarctica should be left alone, as the last real wilderness on our planet.

The southern part of the world has its winter while the northern part has summer. Polar regions stay dark for the whole day at midwinter, and stay light during the night at midsummer.

Walruses are big blubbery animals with flippers and long tusks, which they use to scrape clams off the seabed. They swim in bitterly cold Arctic waters.

Ships entering **polar waters** must be strengthened so that they can smash their way through floating ice.

The big tails of **whales** are called flukes. Many kinds of whale come to feed in polar waters.

Emperor penguins are Antarctic birds. They cannot fly, but they are brilliant swimmers.

Many different kinds of **seal** breed in polar waters. They gather in large numbers on rocks, ice-floes and beaches.

Up to nine-tenths of an **iceberg** may be under water. They are a hazard to shipping.

ATLANTIC OCEAN

Permanent Extent of Sea Ice

INDIAN OCEAN

Drake Passage

WEDELL SEA

Coats Land

Maud Land

Enderby Land

Cape Darnley

Antarctic Peninsula

Ronne Ice Shelf

South Pole

GREATER ANTARCTICA

Vinson Massif▲ 5,410m

LESSER ANTARCTICA

TRANSANTARCTIC MTNS.

Wilkes Land

Ross Ice Shelf

Erebus 3,794m▲

ROSS SEA

PACIFIC OCEAN

Index

Acknowledgements

The publishers wish to thank the artists wh
have contributed to this book:
Martin Camm, John James, Gill Platt, Terr
Riley, Peter Sarson, Roger Smith, Mike
White, Alison Winfield

All photographs used in the First Atlas are
from MKP Archives